Kevin M

London's Country

Capital Transport

Front cover: A line of RTs led by RT 4768, with one in Green Line livery at the rear, stand outside Epsom Station to take the Derby Day crowds to the racecourse in June 1965. The special race day service, the 406F, still runs today despite the fact that the other 406 suffix routes (A-E) have long since vanished. Today, this open-air scene has changed radically, the station entrance having been incorporated into a high-rise development. (Michael Wickham collection)

Back cover: The 317A operated by Hemel Hempstead (Two Waters) garage was one of many uneconomic rural routes operated by LCBS despite conversion to OPO as early as 1956. The route traversed attractive Hertfordshire countryside in the shadow of the Chiltern Hills and close to the National Trust's Ashridge Estate. This view of RF 92 in April 1975 (a month before its withdrawal) shows the vehicle in Nettleden Road, Little Gaddesden, outside the Bridgewater Arms Hotel. The premises are named after the third Duke of Bridgewater who owned the Ashridge Estate and pioneered the construction of canals, hence his nickname of the "Canal Duke". He is buried in Little Gaddesden. (Mike Harris)

First published 2020

ISBN 978 1 85414 447 8

Published by Capital Transport Publishing Ltd
www.capitaltransport.com

Printed in the EU

Title Page: RF 598 crosses the River Wey over Town Bridge at the foot of Guildford's historic High Street on 9 May 1968 on its way to Farnham Road bus station. The bridge is now pedestrianised and the buildings closest to the bus have been demolished for the widening of Millbrook (A281). Route 425 from Dorking originated in 1914 as an Aldershot & District Traction Company (A&D) service which initially reached Leatherhead and subsequently Aldershot. In 1919, it became A&D route S and was renumbered 25 in the following year. In 1928, the Dorking – Guildford section became jointly operated by A&D and the East Surrey Traction Company (later London General Country Services). A&D ceased its involvement upon the creation of LT in 1933, when the route was renumbered 425. (W Ryan)

Above: Making its way along the A22 is LT-liveried RML 2317 working a 409 service from West Croydon to the southerly outpost of Forest Row, a destination which ceased to be served by LCBS when the route was cut back to East Grinstead in October 1979. A bus carrying the number RML 2317 is still going strong. After withdrawal at Godstone in 1977, it was repurchased by LT, painted red, and put back into service in 1978. It is currently owned by the Brighton & Hove Bus Company, carries Thomas Tilling livery and is used for tours and special workings, eg the Sea Front Service. (John Herting/Online Transport Archive)

INTRODUCTION

This colour album presents an opportunity to step back from the bustle of London's city and suburban streets and take a relaxed ride around those parts of the Home Counties which were served by London Transport's (LT's) Country Buses and Green Line coaches (until 1 January 1970) and then by London Country Bus Services (LCBS), a newly formed subsidiary of the National Bus Company (NBC). The abbreviation LT in this book covers the London Passenger Transport Board formed in 1933, the London Transport Executive, a nationalised organisation created in 1948 and its successors. Up to 2000 these bodies used the branding "London Transport".

In LT's era, the Country Area was synonymous with dark green, officially Lincoln green, vehicles. Soon after LCBS inherited LT's green-liveried fleet the Company introduced a slightly lighter shade of green which most of its newer types received and also created its own logo to be carried on its existing and new fleet. However, this colour scheme and logo were quickly superseded by NBC Leaf Green with Corporate branding. Both these liveries are outside the scope of this book which depicts only vehicles painted in Lincoln green which LCBS took many years to eradicate on some of its older vehicles. However, on the transfer of the Country and Green Line fleet, LCBS were generally quick to remove evidence of previous LT ownership.

Although some of the inherited fleet received external facelifts many looked increasingly care worn and neglected over the years. The Company had not intended to retain these vehicles for long because they were committed to 100% one-person operation (OPO), originally referred to as one-man operation (OMO). Although they introduced new OPO types, most of which were not painted Lincoln green, a combination of factors such as vehicle unreliability and shortage of spares militated against the withdrawal of elderly stalwarts such as the RT and RF types, many of which were still in Lincoln green. The increasingly tired appearance of some during the 1970s was often exacerbated by ill-fitting or damaged route blinds. London Country appointed the first female driver at Swanley garage in 1972.

The photographs in this book have been arranged geographically, starting with the most eastern locations south of the Thames, then proceeding in a clockwise direction and ending with the most eastern locations north of the Thames.

London's Lincoln green buses and coaches, many of which have been preserved, are much loved and I hope readers will enjoy this collection of largely unpublished material.

Kevin McCormack
Ashtead, Surrey

The AEC Swifts were ordered by LT but delivered to LCBS. This picture depicts SM 521 setting off from Dartford garage (Priory Road) on 9 August 1977 on an afternoon peak hour working of route 401. This bus entered service at Dartford in July 1971 and remained there until March 1978, some two years before its withdrawal. Apart from the placing of an advertisement on the offside, this vehicle looks much the same as on the day of its entry into service six years earlier. Its Lincoln green livery looks smart, no LCBS logo is displayed on the front and it retains its gold fleet number although the last digit is missing, transforming it into SM 52. The 401 was RT-operated until conversion to OPO in July 1971, mainly using Swifts and occasionally RFs, although a few crew journeys continued. (Chris Evans)

Northfleet provided buses for the main trunk route 480 but various shorts were worked out of Dartford and Swanley garages. However, Dartford buses lacked via blinds for these services which accounts for Dartford-based RT 4050 showing only the route number and destination (Horns Cross) in this view taken in July 1971 in the centre of Dartford. This vehicle resided at the garage from August 1968 to February 1972. It was sold in December 1972 and became a courtesy bus for the Sheraton Hotel at Heathrow. (Fred Ivey)

Probably the most unusual Lincoln green buses operated by LT were the five members of the TT class. These Ford Thames Trader vehicles with Strachans bodywork were specially designed to carry bicycles and riders through the Dartford Tunnel beneath the River Thames, linking this part of Kent with Purfleet in Essex. The buses were based at Dartford garage but owned by the Tunnel Authority and entered service in November 1963. However, as evidenced in this view of TT 5, the service was rarely used and from April 1964 only one bus was operated. Even this was uneconomic and the service was withdrawn in October 1965, replaced by an on-call arrangement using a Land Rover towing a trailer. TT4 is the sole survivor and has become a long-term restoration project. (Alan Mortimer)

In the early 1960s when OPO double deckers were not yet permitted, LT were considering the options for a new Country Area bus and borrowed a Park Royal-bodied lowbridge AEC Renown for evaluation purposes. The vehicle was road tested from February to June 1963 on Northfleet's busy route 480 from Erith to Denton via Dartford and Gravesend. Despite being painted in Lincoln green, it carried no fleet name or number (although it does now in preservation) but was unofficially designated RX 1. The bus was subsequently returned to AEC. It failed to impress LT and the more expensive Routemaster type was chosen instead for Country Area work. Route 480 still runs today over part of the original Kent route. (Alan Mortimer)

When this picture was taken outside Dartford garage on 29 March 1970, three months had elapsed since LT surrendered its Country Bus operations, yet there is scarcely any evidence of the transfer to LCBS. The garage still bears the former owner's name and the LT bullseye motif is in abundance, not least on the radiator badges of the two identifiable buses, ex-Green Line RT 1021 and, on the garage forecourt, RT 3054. Dartford garage was built by Maidstone & District Motor Services in 1927 but had to be surrendered when LT was formed in 1933 with a defined and largely exclusive operating area, which included Dartford. The premises closed in January 1986 when they were replaced by a new garage built nearby. (David Christie)

In the early days of London Country, RT 3886 is seen preparing to leave the bus stop in Bourne Road, Bexley, at its junction with Thanet Road and Albert Road. On the left is Bexley Public Library which opened in 1899 and continues to serve the local community today. The 401A was primarily to serve Joydens Wood Estate with journeys both from the Bexleyheath direction and Dartford direction, the latter being mostly positioning. Swifts took over the route in July 1971 and RT 3886, which was based at Dartford garage from February 1968 to February 1972, was withdrawn in June 1972 and exported to Canada. The extra tall finial on the bus stop is created by a telegraph pole in the background! (Fred Ivey)

This picture taken in March 1974 depicts Swanley's RT 4740 at Wilmington on a 477 service from Dartford and Swanley to Crockenhill. Interestingly, it is still possible today to catch a 477 at Wilmington and make the same journey. Indeed, it was even possible to do this back in 1922 when East Surrey started its S7 service! The original bus numbered RT 4740 was one of those stored for some four years before entering service in March 1958. The anticipated expansion of Country Area services through, for example, the creation of more new towns had not occurred and the downturn in bus usage arising from increased private car ownership had not been anticipated either. Consequently, LT found itself having ordered too many RTs but the surplus vehicles enabled earlier post-war members of the RT family to be sold on to other operators. (Peter Plummer)

This is one of the 43 long and luxurious Routemaster coaches (RCLs), which were introduced in 1965 to compete with the electrified suburban train services between Essex and Liverpool Street. This strategy might have worked if the overcrowded and uncomfortable steam trains had not been replaced by new electric units from 1960. In reality these vehicles arrived on the scene too late. Commuters preferred the trains and patronage on Green Line services was in any case in decline. Green Line route 739, introduced in April 1978, was a short lived service which operated between Victoria and Brands Hatch on motor racing days only. By the time this photograph was taken at Swanley on 16 July 1978 all the RCLs had been removed from regular Green Line operation and this example reverted to LT in October 1978. It was scrapped in 1984. (Peter Plummer)

The 452 route was latterly a Saturdays only working from Dartford to West Kingsdown (Portobello Inn). The pub, which is on the corner of London Road (A20) and Fawkham Road, survives today unlike the route which was withdrawn as early as 20 February 1971. The route number was subsequently re-used for a Windsor to Uxbridge service. In 1953, new GS buses had replaced crew-operated T class single deckers on the 452 but the reign of GSs ended when OPO RFs took over on 13 May 1959. Seen here in West Kingsdown on 13 May 1967 is RF 655 whose operational career ended in March 1977 and which was later sold for scrap. (David Christie)

Ex-Green Line modernised RF 176 hurries through Otford on a 401 service from Sevenoaks to Belvedere on 18 June 1974. The route was shared between Dartford and Swanley garages and this picture was taken during the vehicle's five month stay at Swanley before its final transfer to Dartford from where it was withdrawn in June 1975 and sold for scrap. The origin of this route lay with East Surrey's S1 service which began operation between Dartford and Sevenoaks in September 1922, becoming the 401 in December 1924. Over ensuing years, the routeing has changed and today's 401, operated by red buses, includes only the Belvedere to Bexleyheath section of the 1974 service. (Peter Plummer)

In order to update the image of the Green line coach services, most of which were operated by fifteen-year old RFs, LT decided to trial the modernisation of its RF coach fleet by redesigning an example, RF 136. The prototype, seen here in London Road, Sevenoaks (A224) at the stop adjacent to Tubs Hill Parade, entered service in March 1966. The modifications were deemed a success and as a result a further 174 RFs were modernised from August 1966 to July 1967. However, RF 136 differed from the remainder by having rounded wheel arches as well as unpainted front wheel nut rings and rear wheel discs. RCLs succeeded RFs on the 704 service during 1966 and AEC Reliances (RPs) took over in 1972. On 28 April 1979 the route was split, the Windsor-Victoria section remaining the 704 while the Victoria-Tunbridge Wells portion was renumbered 706. (Alan Mortimer)

LCBS and Maidstone & District share Sevenoaks bus station on 23 October 1971. In the foreground are two Dunton Green RFs, the one on the left (RF 560) having been transferred from Dartford earlier in the year. That accounts for the radiator cap flap still displaying the LT bullseye, although the London Transport wording in the centre will have been painted out. Dartford garage initially seemed reluctant to paint over the flap, unlike Dunton Green, as evidenced by RF 592. Route 431A represented a slight variation of route 431 because, instead of covering the Orpington station to Halstead section via Chelsfield, the 431A travelled via Green Street Green. Both RFs were sold for scrap in the mid-1970s. (David Christie)

This picturesque setting at Ide Hill has not changed over the years, apart from the influx of traffic, and the Cock Inn (shown as the terminus on the 404 blind) is still open. Its pub sign can be seen in the background. Route 404 used to operate between Shoreham village and Sevenoaks but this picture was taken in LCBS days after the route was extended to Ide Hill. RFs took over from 9T9s on the 404 in September 1953 and this route inaugurated the operation of LCBS's first four Bristol LH6s (BL 1-4) in October 1973, replacing the RFs. The bus featured here is RF 236 and the RF bearing this fleet number and registration started life as a Green Line coach, being downgraded to a bus in 1967. (Mike Harris)

As a stop-gap pending the delivery of Country RFs from 1953, LT ordered thirty AEC Regal IIIs (15T13s) with bodies by Mann Egerton which entered service in 1948. By 1956, their work was drying up due to the influx of RFs and the trend towards placing double deckers on former single deck routes for economy purposes, enabling timetable reductions. In that year, the first three 15T13s were withdrawn and this process continued until only a handful remained in 1960. T 787 was in service at Crawley, where this photograph was taken, and normally worked the 426. Its use there ceased in August 1962 and it then moved to Abbey Wood for staff bus duties until April 1963 when it was withdrawn. Most of the class took a one-way journey to Ceylon (Sri Lanka) but T 792 was saved and is the only survivor. (M Taylor/Online Transport Archive)

LCBS's fleet of Swifts was augmented in 1971 by fifteen "Welsh" Swifts which were classified SMW. The first three, the only ones with Willowbrook dual doorway bodies, were acquired second-hand because these had already seen service with South Wales Transport in 1969. All three were sent to Crawley where there was a need for additional buses due to the expanding New Town and the transfer of some Southdown services from 24 April 1971. This view of SMW 3 in its original embellished condition is taken at Crawley bus station. The bus is working a circular service numbered 479A (the 479 travelled in the opposite direction). These routes were previously Southdown 79 and 79A. SMW 3 was withdrawn in January 1981. (Barry Le Jeune)

This Merlin, MBS 413, pictured at East Grinstead on a 434 service to Edenbridge, differs from the fully seated version with the unpopular low driving position by having the higher driving position and is a standee bus. It contains only 25 seats and has provision for 48 standing passengers. This bus, which was delivered in November 1968, spent almost its entire working life at Crawley garage and was withdrawn in February 1980. It is seen outside the High Street branch of the largely forgotten National Provincial Bank and the building is now occupied by an Italian restaurant. (Alan Mortimer)

This view depicts RT 974 at the Carfax, Horsham in August 1966 operating a short service on the 405A Horsham-Redhill route. The blind states Roffey Corner and Horsham via Littlehaven. Horsham was LT's most southerly destination and was also served by Southdown and Aldershot & District. Carfax is often regarded as having taken its name from the Norman word meaning a place where four roads meet. The section where RT 974 is standing is now pedestrianised and the buildings replaced. The vehicle was withdrawn in August 1971 as a red bus. It was then exported to France. (Michael Wickham collection)

With Green Line services flourishing in the 1950s, partly due to the reliability and comfort provided by the RF coaches introduced in 1951, the original fleet of 263 needed enlarging. Consequently, LT adapted an additional 35 RFs for Green Line work including 19 Country Area buses such as the vehicle at that time numbered RF 518 which became RF 299 in March 1956. By the mid 1960s, the requirement for RF coaches had reduced as Green Line services contracted and only 175 were modernised. RF 299 seen here was relegated in due course to bus work and is working a Crawley local service, the 426A from Ifield to Pound Hill. In this view, it is in West Green with a full load heading for Crawley town centre, as it turns out of Ewhurst Road into West Green Drive. (Alan Mortimer)

Conscious that many provincial bus operators in the early 1960s were using front entrance, rear engine double deckers such as Leyland Atlanteans and Daimler Fleetlines, LT decided to buy some for evaluation purposes. Favouring the Atlanteans, LT bought 50 of these and classified them as XAs but also bought eight Fleetlines (the XF class). The XAs were tested against the XFs and RMLs and performed the worst. In 1973 they were sold to Hong Kong while the XFs soldiered on. Allocated to East Grinstead from the outset in September 1965 the XFs remained there for their service lives apart from brief periods in Central London for comparative trials. They were normally used on former RT route 424 from East Grinstead to Reigate, part of which involved travelling along rural lanes, as pictured here with XF 3 on a short working to Copthorne in LCBS days. This bus was withdrawn in December 1981, making it the last ex-LT bus in LCBS service. It is now preserved, along with XF 1. (E Shepherd/ London Bus Museum collection)

With the introduction of the 1965/66 winter timetable on 3 October 1965, RTs on routes 409, 410 and 411 were replaced by new RMLs. This resulted in alterations to services based on the provision of larger buses, but fewer of them. However, there were insufficient new RMLs available and, since the shortfall could not be met by RTs due to the rescheduling, seventeen new red RMLs from a batch numbered 2278-2305 were drafted in from October 1965, based at Godstone. These vehicles then enjoyed rural surroundings for two to three months until more green RMLs became available and they were then dispatched to the Central Area. This view at West Croydon bus station depicts two new buses, green RML 2336, with red RML 2303 behind. The former was acquired by LT in October 1979 and was exported to Nova Scotia in 2010. RML 2303 was exported to a different part of Canada two years later. (Fred Ivey)

The replacement of RTs by RMLs on the 409 in October 1965 was intended to be a long term arrangement but a severe shortage of Routemaster parts in the mid 1970s created major operational problems for LCBS. Three ex-Southdown Leyland PD3s ("Queen Marys") were purchased in 1975 and helped out on the 409 for some twelve months until sold. However, vehicle shortages at Godstone persisted and occasional RT operation occurred as depicted here at Purley Cross on 24 February 1977. Working a peak hour service in fading light, heavily laden RT 986 is making the marathon journey from West Croydon to Forest Row a few weeks before the vehicle's withdrawal. The 409 originated as East Surrey's route S9 in 1922 when it went as far as Uckfield. (Chris Evans)

The Country Area's first Express service was introduced on 14 December 1955. This was a Monday to Friday morning and evening peak hour service on the 403 between West Croydon and Chelsham. RTs were used from the outset but by 1978 this limited stop service was in the hands of ex-Green Line RMC and RCL coaches. The basic 403 service became fully OPO in March 1979 with the arrival of Leyland Atlanteans (AN class) but the 403 Express remained crew-worked until August 1980. On 29 April 1976, the 403 Express had RT 1015 in charge when photographed at Sanderstead. This bus, in presentable condition for the period, had only been transferred to Chelsham in the previous month and was withdrawn just a few days after this working. It was then sold for scrap. (Peter Plummer)

The last RF built as a Country Area bus to remain in service was Chelsham's RF 684. Its other claim to fame was that, until its withdrawal in May 1978, it had remained in Lincoln green livery. As seen here on 21 April 1977, this bus still had hill climbing abilities as it heads up Westhall Road, Upper Warlingham, with the railway station of that name in the background. Unfortunately, as with many ex-LT RTs and RFs in LCBS days, it has a blind display problem because the route number (453) is missing. Unlike many neighbouring routes, the 453 was not a former East Surrey service, having commenced operation on 21 February 1934 under LT auspices. Following withdrawal RF 684 was sold and cannibalised, eventually going for scrap in April 1989. (Chris Evans)

Although Swifts took over from RTs on route 453 in May 1971 and the route was officially converted to OPO two months later, some crew operation remained until full OPO working took place in August 1980. On 16 August 1976, another tidy Chelsham RT was still in use, this time RT 1027, seen at Caterham station, terminus of a branch line from Purley. This vehicle had been transferred to Chelsham in March 1976 but had only a few weeks of operational life remaining when photographed, as it was withdrawn in the following month and sold for scrap in January 1977. The Caterham station building shown in this picture was built in 1899 and has yet to receive British Rail branding. The electric services advertised on the station awning started in 1928. (Peter Plummer)

Returning to the 403 which still operates today (with red buses), this route originated in 1921 as East Surrey's S3 and became the 403 in 1924. From 1950, the route was synonymous with RTs and although these were largely superseded by Routemasters in later years it was some 28 years before the last RT ran on the 403. The use of RFs on this route, as evidenced in this view of RF 684, was however uncommon, particularly in LT days. The location of this picture is Chelsham garage which was opened by East Surrey in 1925 and extended in 1931. This work included increasing the height of the existing building to accommodate double-deckers. The garage closed in 1990 and its existence is commemorated on a blue plaque attached to the supermarket subsequently built on the site. (John Herting/Online Transport Archive)

In terms of buildings and road layout, this 1968 view in Westerham is one of the most unaltered scenes portrayed in the book. Conversely, the 403 service has been subject to several changes over the years as part of a rationalisation of routes serving the same places. For example, the 403 service shown here as running between Wallington and Tonbridge, was cut back from 3 July 1971 to Chelsham with short extensions to Farleigh, Warlingham Park Hospital and Tatsfield. At the same time, a revised 403A service was introduced to operate between West Croydon and Tonbridge. Back in 1937-1938, the route was extremely long, going from Leatherhead to Tonbridge, albeit operated in two overlapping sections. Chelsham-based RT 3121 is the subject of this picture but the reason for its being parked outside the George and Dragon with the crew posing in front is apparently because it was running ahead of schedule when it reached Westerham. (E Shepherd/London Bus Museum)

Seen at Westerham working the 410 service from Bromley to Reigate is Godstone-based RLH 6 from a class of 76 AEC Low Height Regent IIIs. The first twenty including this one were from a cancelled Midland General order and were distinguishable from the remainder by their chrome radiators and raised roof ventilators. Low height double deckers replaced open top ones on this route in 1934 and, in the days before legislation allowed long single deckers, the only economic means of carrying more passengers on a busy route when the bridge was only slightly too low for an RT or standard STL was to provide a low height double decker. RLH 6 entered service in 1950 and was withdrawn at Godstone garage in November 1964. The vehicle then worked for Samuel Ledgard of Leeds for some two years before being exported to the USA in August 1968. (M Taylor/Online Transport Archive)

The RLHs on the 410 were replaced by RTs on 4 November 1964 when the route was diverted away from the offending low bridge at Oxted station, much to the irritation of the local community. After initially refusing, the local council responded to increased pressure to lower the road under the bridge in 1965, enabling the 410 to revert to its original routeing but now with high bridge buses. This picture was taken during the transition from RT to RML operation at Godstone in October 1965. Red RML 2293 was loaned for only a matter of weeks before it was transferred to the Central area. It was eventually withdrawn in 2004 and sold, becoming a mobile café. The vehicle originally numbered RT 4748 entered service in March 1958 after some four years of storage. The final RT 4748 was sold for scrap in 1971. (Peter Plummer collection)

RML 2319 looks magnificent as it sets off from Godstone to Bromley North on route 410 in October 1965 when brand new into service. The garage code shows RG, ie Reigate, rather than Godstone. Both garages provided buses for the 410 and 411 whereas the 409 was shared between Godstone and East Grinstead. Daimler Fleetlines (AF class) replaced the RMLs on the 410 in February 1972. In the background of this photograph is Godstone Garage on Eastbourne Road (A22) which was opened by East Surrey in 1925 and extended in 1928 (when the roof was also raised) and again in 1931. It was closed in 1990 in the same year that the 410 was withdrawn. RML 2319, following its transfer to LCBS in 1970, was repurchased by LT in 1977 but never ran again, being cannibalised for parts. (Peter Plummer collection)

As evidenced in this view, Godstone was served by Green Line coaches in October 1965 when the RMLs worked bus routes 409, 410 and 411. One can be seen in the background on the garage forecourt, above which an air raid siren is visible. These former wartime features were kept operational for Civil Defence purposes during the Cold War. The coach, RF 45, is carrying an impressive load of passengers on its journey from Hemel Hempstead to East Grinstead, a service which was converted to OPO in 1969. Eight years later the northern terminus was extended to Aylesbury following the withdrawal of the 706 and in 1978 the 708 itself was curtailed to run only from Aylesbury to Victoria. RF 45 was modernised in November 1966 and remained in service until July 1976, after which it was sold for scrap. (Alan Mortimer)

The photographer of RT 4497 in June 1966 did not know that he had pictured probably the most famous bus in the world, currently viewed by thousands of people every year! Although its appearance has changed, the vehicle still carries its original registration number, OLD 717. This is none other than the triple-deck Harry Potter Knight Bus. In this view it is meandering through the St John's Conservation Area in Redhill (named after the church in the background) on local Reigate/Redhill route 430 This was the first Country Area route to have its RTs replaced by Autofare-equipped Merlins in November 1968. Following transfer to LCBS, RT 4497 was one of 34 surplus RTs bought back by LT as temporary support for its ailing fleet and all resumed operation in red livery in September 1972 although this particular vehicle only ran for eight months with LT before withdrawal. In this view, it has just passed The Elm Shades pub in Pendleton Road which is now The Pendleton, a burger bar. (Roy Hobbs/ Online Transport Archive)

RT 4198 and modernised RF 78 stand on the forecourt of Reigate bus garage in May 1967. This garage in Lesbourne Road was built for East Surrey in 1931-2 to replace its small garage in neighbouring Bell Street. By the time of completion, the Company had changed its name to London General Country Services after absorbing services west and north of London where the name of East Surrey seemed inappropriate. However, the new name was short-lived, lasting only from January 1932 until July 1933 when the Company was subsumed into LT. The garage, which is Grade II listed, closed in 1996 and, in the absence of an offer to occupy the whole building, part of it (mainly the section behind the RF) was demolished to make way for a low height office block called the Omnibus Building. The remainder has been converted into a children's nursery, with the two sets of concertina doors retained. (Roy Hobbs/Online Transport Archive)

Pictured in October 1965, Daimler Fleetline XF 6 is leaving London Road, Reigate and turning into High Street past the Red Cross Inn on its way to East Grinstead on a 424 service. At that time OPO working was not permitted on double deckers. However, LT introduced experimental OPO working in October 1966, running the XFs (and the XAs against which they were being evaluated) with crews during peak hours and as OPO single deckers for the rest of the time, with the upstairs blocked off with a lockable door. XF 6 had three significant periods away from East Grinstead between September 1965 and withdrawal in December 1979. From April to July 1966 and June 1967 to March 1969 it was allocated to the Central Area. Then in December 1969 it was converted to OPO and painted blue and silver, along with XA 7 and XA 8, to operate on the new Blue Arrow services at Stevenage, returning to East Grinstead in February 1973. (Roy Hobbs/Online Transport Archive)

Passengers board two RFs in October 1965 at the Red Cross stands in Reigate. Red RF 427, on loan to the Country Area, is heading southwards on a 447 service from Merstham to Redhill while Country RF 270 prepares to set off for Newdigate via Dorking on route 439. The vehicle originally bearing the number RF 270 entered service as a Green Line coach in August 1952 and was downgraded to an OPO bus in September 1965. Withdrawn in March 1972, it passed through the hands of various owners before being broken up for spares. The original RF 427 entered service in February 1953 and was converted to OPO in March 1965. Some Central Area RFs spent quite long periods on loan to the Country Area and LCBS but RF 427's change of scenery only lasted a few weeks and it was back in Kingston in the following month. Withdrawn in November 1976, the bus was subsequently sold for scrap. (Roy Hobbs/Online Transport Archive)

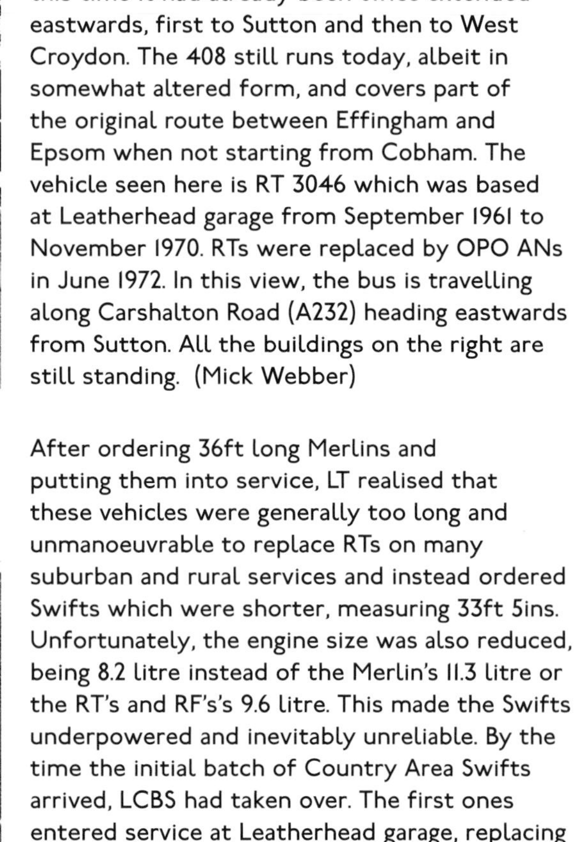

The 408 was another long route which at one time ran from Guildford to Warlingham Park Hospital or Farleigh. It originated in November 1921 as East Surrey's Epsom-Guildford S6B service which was renumbered S8 in the following year and became the 408 in 1924. By this time it had already been twice extended eastwards, first to Sutton and then to West Croydon. The 408 still runs today, albeit in somewhat altered form, and covers part of the original route between Effingham and Epsom when not starting from Cobham. The vehicle seen here is RT 3046 which was based at Leatherhead garage from September 1961 to November 1970. RTs were replaced by OPO ANs in June 1972. In this view, the bus is travelling along Carshalton Road (A232) heading eastwards from Sutton. All the buildings on the right are still standing. (Mick Webber)

After ordering 36ft long Merlins and putting them into service, LT realised that these vehicles were generally too long and unmanoeuvrable to replace RTs on many suburban and rural services and instead ordered Swifts which were shorter, measuring 33ft 5ins. Unfortunately, the engine size was also reduced, being 8.2 litre instead of the Merlin's 11.3 litre or the RT's and RF's's 9.6 litre. This made the Swifts underpowered and inevitably unreliable. By the time the initial batch of Country Area Swifts arrived, LCBS had taken over. The first ones entered service at Leatherhead garage, replacing RTs on the Bookham-Kingston 418 service on 27 June 1970. In this view, SM 112 is entering the Wood Street terminus alongside Kingston station. The scene is unrecognisable today. All the buildings have been replaced and if SM 112 were to reverse now it would disappear the wrong way down an underpass! (Alan Snatt)

In LCBS days modernised RFs normally had their waist bands painted light green or canary yellow but a few received NBC white. One such example was Leatherhead's RF 54, seen outside its home garage on 2 July 1977 working an Esher – Boxhill 416 service. This route originated on 8 April 1925 as East Surrey's 408D service (renumbered 416 later that year) running from West Croydon to Esher via Leatherhead and Oxshott, thereby covering part of the LCBS section. RF 54, which was withdrawn in October 1977 and sold for scrap, was one of three RFs drafted into Leatherhead in January/February 1977 to replace BNs transferred to Harlow pending the arrival of more BNs to Leatherhead later in the year. (Chris Evans)

Winding its way around the lanes of the North Downs in Surrey on its way from Esher is RF 621, heading for the alternative 416 southern terminus of Tadworth station instead of Boxhill (Greenacres). RF-operated route 416 was an early OPO conversion from crew operation, a change which took effect in October 1957. Coincidentally, this was the same month that RF 621 was converted to OPO but the vehicle was not allocated to Leatherhead until January 1963. It continued to work from there until January 1976 and was sold for scrap two months later. In this view looking north, the bus is in Church Lane approaching Headley Heath at the junction with Nut Ash Lane/Leech Lane (B 2033). (Alan Mortimer)

To cater for ramblers visiting Leith Hill East Surrey introduced route 33 from Dorking (North) station to the Plough Inn at Coldharbour in April 1930. As it operated beyond the area covered by the Metropolitan Police which had become responsible for London bus services in 1924, the service was not initially required to have a 4xx route number but LT renumbered it 433 in August 1934, simultaneously extending it to Ranmore Common. Never a busy service, the route was withdrawn on 5 October 1968. Guy Specials had replaced Leyland Cubs in December 1953 and in this view, GS 42, which later became the last GS to operate in public service, has climbed up Ranmore Road and reached the junction with North Downs Way, with St Barnabas church spire behind. The bus would then continue along Ranmore Common Road and terminate in Dog Kennel Green, almost in Effingham. (Alan Mortimer)

RT 4767, on Route 418 from Kingston to Bookham station, descends Bridge Street, Leatherhead, in August 1965. At the bottom is the bridge over the River Mole where a 418 service came to grief in 1930. East Surrey S type double decker No 92 crashed into the brick parapet and nearly ended up in the river! In this view, the buildings are still extant but the Oddfellows Hall and Halifax Building Society buildings are now private houses. Despite the replacement of RTs by OPO Swifts on the 418 in 1970 RTs continued to work the route occasionally due to the unreliability of the Swifts. The Bookham to Epsom section of the old 418 now forms part of today's 479 service from Guildford but does not run northwards beyond Epsom. (E Shepherd/London Bus Museum)

This resplendent vehicle, RF 544, was based at Guildford garage from August 1967 until withdrawal in January 1973, whereupon it was sold for scrap. It is standing in London Road, Dorking (A24), just beyond the junction with Station Approach and Lincoln Road. The station in question is the former London, Brighton & South Coast Railway's Dorking station which, following the creation of the original Southern Railway in 1923, was renamed Dorking North in that year to distinguish it from the SR's other two Dorking stations, Deepdene (a short walk away) and Dorking Town, both on the former South Eastern & Chatham Railway's Tonbridge to Reading line. It reverted to its original name in 1968 and all three stations remain open. (Alan Mortimer)

The 412 was a rural route from Dorking to Sutton Abinger (The Volunteer) and this photograph of RF 630 was taken at one of the villages served, Holmbury St Mary. The service began as East Surrey's route 22 (Dorking-Holmbury) in June 1927 and was renumbered 412 in October 1934. From the start, a bus was outstationed at the Royal Oak at Holmbury and, surprisingly, this arrangement lasted until November 1975, twelve months after Bristol BNs had replaced RFs. When the 433 was withdrawn on 5 October 1968, the 412 was extended from Dorking North station to cover the Ranmore Common section and the route was extended again, this time at the opposite end, to serve Cranleigh and Ockley from 1 September 1979. (Michael Wickham collection)

Nowadays, this bus (RLH 50) is called Delila, painted in LT red and currently available for hire from Roadtrips of Marlborough. However, this Marlborough is on South Island, New Zealand! From December 1964 to July 1970 the bus was based at Addlestone and was one of seventeen RLHs transferred to LCBS for low height routes operated by Addlestone and Guildford garages. These services saw the RLHs ousted by Swifts on 1 August 1970 although, ironically, the 420 from West Byfleet to Woking station via the Sheerwater Estate (where this picture was taken) was not a lowbridge route. Indeed it was very short, only some four miles long, and in this view RLH 50 is on a school working to Maybury East Hill. A hand waves at the photographer through the nearside upper front window! However, only a contortionist could do this now because a safety bar has been fitted across the upper part of both windows. (Alan Mortimer)

The 436 was a lowbridge route which ran from Staines to Guildford and there was also a Guildford circular short working from the bus station (Onslow Street) to Burpham (pronounced "Bur-fam"), as seen here. RLH 36 is turning out of Glendale Drive into Winterhill Way, Burpham at a location which is basically unchanged today although the bus stop flag is now on a separate pole rather than attached to the lamp post. The bus was based at Addlestone from January 1966 until its withdrawal in July 1970 and, like RLH 50 on the previous page, it spent a short time with an operator in Upminster. Then, in November 1971 it was exported to Hawaii and eventually scrapped. (Alan Mortimer)

GS 25 meets up with GS 21 and an RF at the top of North Street, Guildford, on its way to Onslow Street bus station as it returns from Peaslake on a 448 working. This route, which reached Ewhurst until November 1955 and apparently required a hacksaw to be carried to deal with any encroaching vegetation in the narrow lanes, was shared with Tillingbourne Valley Services until August 1964 when LT ceased its involvement. Tillingbourne operated other services to remote villages as well as those on the 448 route and purchased thirteen GS buses from LT, including GS 25. All the buildings in this picture have been replaced except the tall one on the right. A pub called The Crown which closed in 1907 used to stand beside this building but was removed for road widening. (Fred Ivey)

LT's Green Line RC class of AEC Reliances turned out to be notoriously unreliable but this did not deter LCBS from ordering 90 updated AEC Reliances with Park Royal bodies in 1971. This RP class of coaches was more successful than their predecessors but still had a relatively short life, replaced on Green Line services by more typical-looking coaches. Although only officially downgraded to bus work in their later days (the last one was withdrawn in 1984) they were used on bus routes even in their early life, as evidenced in this view of RP 53 in The Broadway, Woking. The location is opposite the railway station and the buildings seen here are still in situ. RP 53 was delivered to Addlestone in February 1972 to replace Routemaster coaches on routes 716 and 716A and remained in traditional Green Line livery until September 1974. Following withdrawal in August 1983, the vehicle went to a buyer in Sheffield but was destroyed in a depot fire in November 1985. (Mike Harris)

When viewed from the front the 76 Weymann-bodied RLHs bore a resemblance to an old-style LT bus such as the STL type. However, they looked distinctly provincial from the rear, as demonstrated by RLH 13 on a Guildford-Staines 436 service in Commercial Way, Woking, on 21 April 1968, under the watchful eye of a bus inspector. Five years later a start was made on the rebuilding of the town centre which involved considerable demolition and road alterations. Although most of the buildings seen here, both old and new, have survived, Commercial Way is no longer a through route out of the town. RLH 13 was based at Guildford garage from February 1959 until withdrawal in July 1970 and, after some changes of ownership, was exported to The Netherlands in December 1974. (W Ryan)

As other operators were starting to replace crewed buses with large capacity OPO vehicles LT decided to trial this concept by ordering fifteen AEC Merlins with Strachans bodywork. The first six (XMS 1-6), designed for both seated and standing passengers, were delivered in February 1966 for the Central Area and entered service two months later to operate the first Red Arrow express service in the City and West End. A further nine (XMB 1-9) were fully seated buses for the Country Area and were delivered in April 1966. These were intended for three Addlestone routes but staff refused to operate them. Consequently, they were put into store, all but one of them subsequently being transferred to the Central area and converted into Standee buses to match the original six. This picture shows a newly arrived XMB in store at Addlestone in summer 1966. A Strachans advertisement is displayed in one of the windows. (Bill Cottrell/London Bus Museum)

The seventeen RLHs transferred to LCBS ran for only seven months before being replaced by Swifts. Twelve had been at Addlestone and the remaining five at Guildford for the shared routes. In this view, withdrawal is imminent for RLH 45 standing at Addlestone garage with two trainer RTs behind. However, this was not the end for RLH 45. The bus, now in red livery, lives on as "Daisy" and is currently available for hire from Robbies Double Decker Travel, Auckland, North Island, New Zealand! Addlestone's garage code was WY, believed to stand not for Weybridge or River Wey but for Weymann, because before the garage was opened in June 1936, LT's buses and coaches were kept at Weymann's nearby premises about a mile away. Addlestone garage was demolished in 1997 and the site redeveloped, becoming Gleeson Mews. A brick entrance pillar is all that remains. (John Herting/Online Transport Archive)

Low height RLH 33 travels through Walton-on-Thames, terminus of route 463 from Guildford bus station (Onslow Street), in the last few weeks of RLH operation for LCBS. The last day was 31 July 1970 which was the date of the vehicle's withdrawal. In November 1970, RLH 33 was exported to Hawaii where it was scrapped some thirty years later. In this scene the bus has just pulled out of High Street, entered Hepworth Way and is just about to pass the photographer's wife with her twin buggy. A certain amount of redevelopment has subsequently taken place at this cross roads although the extra -wide pavement remains. Sadly, the historic building on the left has been replaced by something unremarkable. (Martin Jenkins/Online Transport Archive)

This smart-looking vehicle with reduced blind display, RT 3607, was photographed on route 469 (Staines – Virginia Water) on 10 August 1976. The bus had only arrived at Staines garage in June 1976 and was withdrawn at the end of the year, becoming a crew changing room at Leatherhead garage until sold for scrap in June 1978. The 469 had been operated by STLs until November/December 1952 when Staines received new RTs to replace them. Latterly, RFs tended to be used (albeit not on this occasion) until these were replaced by Leyland Nationals in October 1976. RT 3607 is standing in Village Road, Thorpe, just beyond the junction with Coldharbour Lane and opposite the Red Lion pub. The attractive village of Thorpe, between Egham and Chertsey, boasts 38 listed buildings and several historic high brick walls. It is located about a mile away from the former gravel pit now known as Thorpe Park, the popular theme park. (Peter Plummer)

Brand new RTs replaced STLs on the long 441 route from Staines to High Wycombe in 1950 and were themselves replaced by RMLs in October 1972. However, unscheduled use of RTs on the 441 continued, as demonstrated by RT 4495 in this photograph taken in South Street, Staines on 15 May 1976. The bus, a resident of Staines garage, appears in presentable condition apart from the torn blinds at the front. The 441 became an OPO route with the arrival of Leyland Nationals in September 1977. RT 4496 was withdrawn three months after being seen here and was then sold for scrap. A 441 service still exists today, running from Englefield Green to Staines (now known as Staines-upon-Thames) via Egham which therefore covers a short section of the original route. (Peter Plummer)

Between 1950 and 1960 85 RTs received Green Line livery and were used on the Aldgate routes or as Relief coaches across the LT network. Unlike the RMCs and RCLs which succeeded them in 1962 and 1965 respectively, the RTs had no special coach refinements and were indistinguishable from the rest of the class apart from wearing a slight adaptation of Country bus livery and the absence of external advertisements. Although the RTs continued to be used sometimes on Green Line relief work into the 1970s, they were normally found on ordinary bus routes working alongside the standard-liveried Country RTs, as is the case here. RT 979 is pictured on 16 May 1968 climbing Thames Street alongside Windsor Castle on Uxbridge-Windsor route 457. The backdrop to this picture has not changed over the years. (W Ryan)

The 442 from Slough to Farnham Royal via Stoke Green and Stoke Poges, operated by a Windsor-based GS, was one of the routes that was axed following the disastrous bus strike of 1958. This 442 is therefore not to be confused with another route with the same number introduced at High Wycombe in October 1965 and initially also operated by GSs. The Slough 442 had been worked by a variety of bus types prior to Windsor garage receiving three new GSs in July 1954 for both the 442 and 445. Entering service in April 1954 and being sold in January 1964 meant that GS 78's operational life with LT lasted under ten years and it was broken up in 1967. This picture dates from 1955 and was taken at Slough station. (Michael Wickham collection)

Displaying a board stating a minimum fare of one shilling (5p), RT 4769 sets off from Uxbridge bus station with a short journey on the 803 Express to its home garage at Garston (Watford). Before the southern terminus was moved northwards to Maple Cross, this Monday-Friday rush hour service introduced in 1956 operated from Welwyn Garden City station to Uxbridge via New Hatfield and St Albans. This was a journey of 28 miles scheduled to take 85 minutes. The route became OPO in July 1972 when ANs took over. The original RT 4769 was delivered in June 1954 and stored for exactly five years before entering service. The latterday RT 4769 became a Central Area red bus in 1969 and was sold for scrap in September 1976. (John Herting/Online Transport Archive)

Some 441 journeys diverged from the normal route to Beaconsfield and High Wycombe (A355) by serving Hedgerley village. Just beyond the foot of the steep hill into the village was the Brick Mould pub (now a private house) at the junction of Village Lane and Kiln Lane and the bus terminated at the side of the hostelry. In this view dating from 17 August 1976, RT 1009 has climbed the hill and is standing at the cross roads by the One Pin pub (since demolished) before proceeding along One Pin Lane to the junction of Collinswood Road/Beaconsfield Road (Hedgerley Corner). Today, the old signpost has been replaced but the cast iron Hedgerley Hill street sign is still attached to the railings. As seen here, the bus is not running to Staines but is working a short to the Bells of Ouzeley at Old Windsor. RT 1009 was based at Windsor garage from January 1976 to March 1977 when it was withdrawn and exported to the USA where it was converted to open-top. (Peter Plummer)

For those readers who have never heard of Jordans village, Chiltern Railways can provide a clue because the railway station between Gerrards Cross and Beaconsfield is Seer Green & Jordans. The 305 bus route operated between High Wycombe and Uxbridge but on Tuesdays and Friday mornings there was a service for shoppers between Beaconsfield and Jordans village using the 305 number. In this photograph taken in June 1975, two elderly shoppers are just recovering from descending the steep steps of Amersham-based RF 615. Surprisingly, the main 305 route and the twice a week Beaconsfield - Jordans bifurcation are still running, but under a new number, 580. Sadly, RF 615 is no longer running. It was withdrawn at Amersham in February 1976 and sold for scrap. (Mike Harris)

This is Eason Street, High Wycombe in June 1975 and locally-based RML 2440 has just turned out of Crendon Street while working the 326 Micklefield Estate (Woodside Road) – Mill End Road service. RMLs replaced RTs on this route in September 1971 and crew operation ceased following the closure of High Wycombe garage on 30 September 1977. Operation of the 326 was then transferred to Amersham garage and OPO Swifts took over the route. RML 2440 was based at High Wycombe from January 1975 to June 1979 whereupon it was repurchased by LT, painted red and re-entered service. The bus was sold in April 2004 and is now preserved. (Mike Harris)

With the gradual phasing out of the GS class during the 1960s it came as something of a surprise to have a new GS route created on 4 November 1964. This was the 309A working out of Garston garage and operating between Northwood, Rickmansworth and Chorleywood. This covered a section of Green Line route 703 (Wrotham-Amersham) which was withdrawn on the previous day. No additional GS was required for the 309A as there was a GS allocation for the 309 and this service was altered as a result of the new route. The phased introduction of OPO RFs ended GS use on the 309 and 309A on 15 February 1969. Fortunately, the vehicle seen here across the road from Mount Vernon Hospital, GS 15, which entered service in October 1953 and was based at Garston from January 1965 up to withdrawal in February 1969, has been preserved. (Capital Transport)

One of LT's most unusual routes was the 336A which ran between the Loudwater private estate and Rickmansworth Underground station. The service, which was started by the owner of the estate in 1924, was operated from 1953 by a single GS bus allocated to Garston garage (a second was kept as a spare). Until the regular driver, Harry Cross who lived locally, retired in early 1971, the bus was stabled overnight on the estate, thereby avoiding uneconomic trips to Garston except at weekends when it was switched with the spare GS. Mr Cross paid in the fares which he had collected to Rickmansworth station. However, the next 336A driver did not live nearby and the bus had to return to Garston at night. Consequently, LCBS, who had inherited the service, decided to withdraw it, the last day being 30 March 1972, thereby bringing an end to GS public service operation. These pictures depict GS 17 in LT days and GS 42 in LCBS ownership, both taken on the Loudwater Estate. (John Herting/Online Transport Archive; Fred Ivey)

Route 362 began in 1919 as Amersham & District Motor Bus & Haulage Company's route 1 from Ley Hill to High Wycombe via Chesham, Amersham and Holmer Green until this Company was taken over by LT in 1933. In this view RT 3198 is standing opposite its home garage of Amersham (currently the site of a Tesco filling station) during its short stay at that garage between March and June 1968. Interestingly, it is wearing a set of old blinds with upper case lettering. Crew operation of this route ended on 15 February 1971 with the arrival of Swifts, making Amersham the first LCBS garage to be 100% OPO. RT 3198 lives on, but as RT 3238! It has been re-registered as KYY 967 because in its final embodiment RT 3198 consisted of a Green Line body and chassis and has therefore been preserved as an authentic Green Line RT. (Michael Wickham collection)

RF 307 leaves Amersham station on the short-lived 336B route. This Sunday-only service commenced on 8 November 1964 covering part of the withdrawn 703 Green Line route. However, despite being extended from Amersham to Great Missenden on 1 January 1967, the RF-operated 336B only lasted until 2 June 1968. A Country bus originally registered as RF 326 entered service in April 1953 and was another of those which were converted into a Green Line coach in 1956 and given the fleet number, RF 307. Retaining this identity, it became a bus again in 1962. In that year the vehicle was sent to Amersham as a GS replacement and remained at that garage until withdrawal in May 1975, after which it was sold for scrap. Amersham station opened in 1892 and is now the principal western terminus of LT's Metropolitan Line. (Alan Mortimer)

The 398 was a long-established route and over the years had been extended to Chesham and Penn. However, when ex-Green Line modernised RF 193 was photographed in Grove Road, Quill Hall Estate, on the northern outskirts of Amersham, the service only went from the Estate to Beaconsfield (Saracens Head) via Amersham and Coleshill. In fact, the Estate did not have a bus service until 16 October 1957 when it was reached by the 398 and 398A. RF 193 was based at Amersham garage from May 1974 to November 1975 and, following withdrawal in January 1977, was sold for scrap. Before the RFs arrived in 1953 the 398 was operated by Leyland Cubs. Bristol BLs entered service at Amersham in January 1974 and were used on the 398 but Amersham, like so many Country garages, retained some RFs as substitutes for less reliable vehicles. (Mike Harris)

The National Omnibus & Transport Company introduced their route N6 in 1921 and this evolved into LT's Chesham – Watford 336 service. Six National lowbridge buses dating from 1930, with two upper deck sunken gangways producing an island block of three seats, were acquired by LT and used on the 336 until replaced by the first six RLHs (with only one sunken gangway) in 1950. The requirement for reduced height double deckers on the 336 was due to a low bridge (Black Horse Bridge) in Woodside Road (A4154) carrying the Underground tracks between Amersham and Chalfont & Latimer stations. RLH 35 is seen here operating a short journey shortly before the 336 was taken over by RFs in October 1965. This bus was then transferred to Addlestone and in 1970 was sold to Reigate Grammar School. In 1986 it was exported to Basel in Switzerland. (Alan Mortimer)

With a clearly readable road sign in the background RT 611 is standing at the Watford Heath terminus of route 301. This was one of two potential termini for this service in the Watford area, the other being Little Bushey, both being shared with the 302. The origins of the 301 go back to route 145 (Bushey station-Boxmoor) operated by the London General Omnibus Company which became National's N2 in August 1921. In latter days, buses for the 301 were supplied by both Hemel Hempstead (Two Waters) and Tring garages. RT 611 was based at Two Waters garage from June 1972 to May 1975, the latter date coinciding with the OPO conversion of the 301 and 302. The bus was eventually withdrawn in December 1976 and sold for scrap. (Capital Transport)

This is the Little Bushey terminus of routes 301 and 302 in Chiltern Avenue, opposite the junction with Oundle Avenue. Since this photograph was taken in June 1973 the location has not undergone any material change apart from the replacement of the red telephone box with a glass one and the repositioning of the bus stop a few yards back from the junction. The end of RT operation on the 302 should have ceased in May 1975 but RTs deputising for RMLs continued a little longer on the few workings allocated to Garston garage. The subject of this picture, RT 994, was based at Tring, spending from August 1970 to June 1975 at that garage. The bus was withdrawn in January 1977 and sold to a scrap merchant. (Capital Transport)

Introduced on 5 March 1952 to improve Watford local bus services around the expanding Oxhey Estate, the 346A replaced the northern end of the 345 and the southern end of the 332 operating between Kingswood and Oxhey Estate via the Town Centre. The two terminals were linked to form a vast loop to facilitate MBS working in 1969. As a result of problems with displaying suffixes on the three-track route number blinds as fitted on new Leyland Nationals, LCBS renumbered many routes. New Merlins replaced scheduled RT operation on the 346A on 15 February 1969 and this picture taken in August 1969 depicts Garston-based MBS 284 in the Oxhey Estate. The bus was withdrawn in November 1978 and would then join RTs in the scrapyard. (E Shepherd/London Bus Museum)

As evidenced in this photograph on the Oxhey Estate taken in May 1973 crew operation on the 346A did not end as intended on 15 February 1969. In the 1970s Garston experienced a chronic shortage of serviceable RMLs for their remaining crew-operated routes due to difficulties in obtaining spare parts. Consequently, surplus RTs from other garages were drafted into Garston. Furthermore, some Merlins were dispatched elsewhere to cover for the late delivery of Leyland Nationals, providing more work for Garston's RTs. Five operational ones remained in 1975, working on routes which included the 346A. Four of these buses even lasted into 1977 but not the vehicle shown here, RT 4744, which was withdrawn in March 1975 and sold to a dealer. (Peter Plummer collection)

Route 318 was another converted from crew operation RT to Merlin OPO on 15 February 1969 and this view of MB 100 was taken later in that year. This Garston-based vehicle was delivered in January 1968 as SMM 100F and was registered as VLW 100G in August 1968 since it had not yet entered service. The bus only had a short working life, being withdrawn in January 1980 and then sold for scrap but, unlike the RCs which spent so much time in storage, it was in use for most of that time. In this picture, MB 100 is in St Albans Road, Watford, about to cross the intersection with Langley Road and Station Road. The buildings on the left with their chimney pots are still in situ as are the box junction markings. (Geoffrey Tribe/Online Transport Archive)

The dishonour of being LT's least successful vehicle type probably lies with the fourteen Willowbrook-bodied RC class of Reliance coaches introduced in November 1965. Impressive looking, they were intended as replacements for the aging RF coaches on Green Line services. However, they proved highly unsuccessful and ended up on this work as duplicates for the RFs, the modernisation of which was deemed to be a better proposition. Much of their life was spent in store and in 1974 they were demoted to bus work. From May to September 1969, they were tried out on the airport 727 service when this photograph of St Albans-based RC 7 was taken at the Dome roundabout in Watford, where the A412 intersects the A41 Watford Bypass. RC 7 was withdrawn in January 1977 and sold for scrap. (Geoffrey Tribe/Online Transport Archive)

In this 1969 view, Garston Garage's longest vehicle type (the Merlin) meets its shortest type (the Guy Special). MB 107 was one of six MBs which entered service on 15 February 1969 to operate as OPO vehicles on routes 318, 318A and 335. The vehicle remained at Garston until February 1974 and was withdrawn in May 1978 followed by scrapping. GS 17, along with GS 33, was allocated to the Rickmansworth-Loudwater Estate 336A service (GS operation on the 309 and 309A had ceased on 15 February 1969) but GS 17 was withdrawn in March 1971 following mechanical problems. It was replaced by GS 42 from Garston's training fleet for the remaining twelve months of the 336A's existence. Both GS 17 and GS 42 have since been preserved. (John Herting/Online Transport Archive)

RF 607 climbs up Gallows Hill, Abbots Langley, approaching the junction with Abbots Road in April 1971. Route 322 operated between Hemel Hempstead, where the bus was garaged, and Watford via Kings Langley. RFs took over from 10T10s on this route in September 1953 but the replacement of the RFs was not straightforward. Swifts were the designated substitutes to commence conversion in November 1975 but drivers refused to operate them because of their dual doors. However, they accepted Leyland Nationals and these replaced RFs from 15 May 1976. RF 607 was withdrawn in October 1973 and sold for scrap. The location is largely unchanged today but the road under the narrow bridge is now a single carriageway controlled by traffic lights. The trees, brick wall and lamp posts remain in place. (E Shepherd/London Bus Museum)

RF 571 displays the black masking used to reduce the size of the front blind aperture which some garages adopted for the RF class in the 1970s. This was due to the amount of interworking undertaken by the ultra reliable RF class which required as many routes as possible, albeit in abbreviated form, to be fitted onto the existing roller. The 319 service was shared between Hemel Hempstead and Garston and ran from Watford to Kings Langley with a few journeys to Sarratt. In Kings Langley the service visited the Ovaltine Works, as seen here in August 1974. The Works, which were built in 1927, ceased production in 2002 and have since been converted into luxury flats. RFs were replaced on the 319 in 1976 by Leyland Nationals and RF 571, which was based at Hemel Hempstead from March 1972 to March 1975, went for scrap in June 1975. (Mike Harris)

Tring garage closed on 1 April 1977 along with the contemporaneous withdrawal of Green Line route 706, the Aylesbury section being covered thenceforth by an extension of the 708 from Hemel Hempstead. Tring's operations were then transferred to Hemel Hempstead but, as far as enthusiasts were concerned, Tring went out in a blaze of glory. This was because from June 1976 until 28 January 1977 RT 3530 (succeeded by RT 3631 from September) worked a morning and evening peak hours round trip between Aylesbury and Victoria (and sometimes all the way to Chelsham). This extraordinary Monday to Friday working had probably been the first (and last) semi-regular RT working on a Green Line route for some ten years! This picture of a somewhat empty RT 3530 was taken on 19 August 1976 at Berkhamsted. The bus was withdrawn in January 1977 and sold for scrap. (Peter Plummer)

Another incentive to visit Tring garage was to see the vehicle in this picture: a Strachans-bodied Merlin. Starting life as JLA 57D in 1966, it was re-registered as NHX 15E and finally SMM 15F. Originally allocated fleet number XMB 1, it was quickly renumbered XMB 15. The bus was transferred to Tring in January 1969 and subsequently passed to LCBS. In July 1971 it became MBS 15 and in November 1973, due to certificate of fitness expiry, it was swapped with LT's MBS 4 (originally XMS 4) which was the only Strachans Merlin to have received a full overhaul. LT promptly withdrew MBS 15 and after a period in store sent it for scrapping in March 1977. This view of MBS 15, prior to the exchange, was taken in Tring as the vehicle made its way from Aldbury to Highfield Road on local service 387. (Alan Snatt)

LT created a fleet of 68 standard-length Routemaster coaches for Green Line work based on the prototype, CRL 4. This example, RMC 1504, pictured in 1963, went to Garston when new in November 1962 to replace RFs on route 719 (Victoria-Hemel Hempstead), only to be replaced on this service by RFs in December 1967! After demotion to bus work, the vehicle was repurchased by LT from LCBS in 1980, painted red and used as a trainer. It was scrapped in 1990. This photograph was taken at Leverstock Green, at the junction of Bedmond Road and Leverstock Green Road (A4147). The location looks different today due to the cottages on the left being obscured by trees and the war memorial, unveiled in 1921, having been moved in 1997 to a more tranquil position behind the cottages. (Geoffrey Tribe/Online Transport Archive)

In 1960 LT began to consider potential replacements for the RF type, not anticipating their survival in front line service for another nineteen years! LT liked Grimsby-Cleethorpes Transport's Willowbrook-bodied small Reliances and ordered three new ones from AEC, giving them fleet numbers RW 1-3. So that the practicality of dual doors (one entry, one exit) could be tested on a busy OPO Country Area route they were initially placed on the 322 service from Hemel Hempstead (Highfield) to Watford Junction via Kings Langley station. However, in the early 1960s the dual door concept was relatively novel and drivers objected on the grounds that they had insufficient control over the centre door. The RWs were tried at various garages before returning to Hemel Hempstead in June 1963. Deemed unsuitable for LT, all three were withdrawn in October 1963 and sold to Chesterfield Corporation. This photograph dating from September 1963 depicts RW 3, since preserved, in Lower Road, Nash Mill at the junction with Red Lion Lane. The road has since been realigned to provide for a roundabout at this location. (Geoffrey Tribe/Online Transport Archive)

Hemel Hempstead (Two Waters) garage received eleven auto-fare fitted MBS Merlins to put into service in February 1969 for local routes and this included the replacement of RFs on the 344 (Hemel Hempstead to Grove Hill). RF 578, seen here in St Agnells Lane (opposite Dawley Court) on a winter's day with its side panels covered in slush, arrived at Hemel Hempstead in December 1967, remaining there until withdrawal in October 1972 and ending up with a potato merchant in Perth, Scotland. A major reorganisation of services in the Hemel Hempstead area took place in January 1977, involving the creation of H-prefix routes. The 344 was withdrawn and replaced by the H6 and H14. (John Herting/Online Transport Archive)

When LT was formed in 1933 it started a programme of building large, stylish bus garages. Wallis, Gilbert and Partners were the principal architects commissioned to undertake this work and they designed many well known garages including Addlestone and Amersham and, just prior to LT's creation, Dorking and Windsor, all of which have been demolished. Probably their most spectacular buildings to survive today are Victoria Coach Station and the former Hoover factory in Perivale. The best example of their bus garages was generally regarded as being St Albans at the north end of St Peter's Street. Built in 1936 and discreetly concealed behind a Modernist two-storey office block, it was fronted by a bus station occupied, in this October 1971 view, by RF 661, RT 3891 and Green Line RF 195. Partially concealed in the garage forecourt is RF 54. The garage closed in 1991 and demolished in 1998 to make way for housing despite several attempts to save it. (E Shepherd/London Bus Museum)

RMC 1509 passes St Peter's church in St Albans on its way to Hatfield and Hertford. Behind the cars a bus can be glimpsed in the background where the combined bus station and garage stands. Following the final removal of RMCs from Green Line duty in the late 1960s and early 1970s the class was downgraded to crew operation bus work. RMC 1509 was a resident of Hatfield garage from February 1969 to September 1975 and this type started to replace RTs on the 341 service in March 1972. Crew operation ceased in November 1977 when Leyland Nationals took over but within four years double deckers had returned to the 341 in the form of ANs. RMC 1509 was bought by LT in January 1978 as a non-runner and immediately dispatched for dismantlement and scrapping. (Peter Plummer)

Twelve out of the fifteen Welsh Swifts obtained by LCBS in 1971 were allocated to St Albans. Unlike the first three sent to Crawley which were second-hand, this batch were new buses diverted from South Wales Transport and were fitted with Marshall single doorway bodies. Initially, they had fixed windows but passengers complained about the lack of ventilation so all twelve had opening sections fitted to some windows. This bus is SMW 9 and is pictured on 16 July 1977 in St Peter's Street, St Albans, at the junction with Hatfield Road and Catherine Street. It entered service in January 1972 but, when photographed, had only a few months of service remaining as it was placed in store in January 1978 and disposed of in February 1981. Unlike some of the fifteen, it retained its Lincoln green livery, AEC badge and unpainted aluminium trim to the end. (Chris Evans)

A demoted Green Line coach, RF 101, reaches the terminus of route 382 at the 16th century Goat Inn in Codicote after completing its journey from St Albans garage in August 1973. Although it operated daily except Sundays, the 382 was a somewhat infrequent service with only four return journeys on Mondays-Fridays and six on Saturdays. RF 101 was based at St Albans from May 1972 to October 1973 after which it was withdrawn and sold for scrap. Bristol BLs arrived in June 1973 to replace the RFs but did not start entering service on the 382 until October 1973. The delay was caused by issues relating to the fact that drivers were having to change from buses with pre-selective gearboxes (ie the RFs) to old fashioned manual gearboxes on the new BLs. (John Miller)

LT's discrete Private Hire fleet was disbanded in 1963 due to staff shortages but Country Area garages continued to run tours although these had always been restricted by legislation to the LT operating area. In this view, Northfleet garage's modernised Green Line RF 183 has brought a tour from Gravesend to Whipsnade Zoo near Dunstable. The signage on the bus refers to Whipsnade Park Zoo which appears to be an abbreviation of the full name in use at the time which was Whipsnade Wild Animal Park, opened in 1931. RF 183 was based at Northfleet following modernisation in 1966 and left there in April 1968 for conversion into an OPO bus. In February 1978 it was converted into a tow bus and has since been preserved. The AA Minivan carries a registration from 1965/1966 during the period when vans were replacing the familiar motorcycle combinations. (Michael Wickham collection)

Route 360 operating between Luton and Caddington village managed to escape modernisation until late in the day although it was cut back from Dunstable in 1975. RTs were used exclusively until one duty was taken over by a Leyland National from 22 May 1976 but RTs could still be found on the 360 until 4 September 1976. Three months later the service was transferred to United Counties as a prelude to the closure of Luton garage on 28 January 1977, the first such closure by LCBS. On 8 May 1976 during its five month stay at Luton, RT 3636 was photographed outside All Saints Church in Luton Road, Caddington, displaying a masked destination box. This scene is virtually unaltered today, even down to the iron gate. (Peter Plummer)

GS 65 appears to be well patronised in this picture taken at Hitchin although perhaps this is not surprising since route 386 only ran on Tuesdays, Thursdays and Saturdays and not necessarily covering the whole route. The 386 started at Bishops Stortford and ran to Hitchin via Standon, Buntingford, Stevenage and Great Wymondley. Until its closure on 29 April 1959, Hitchin had a small LT garage but Hertford always provided buses for the 386. This route was converted to GS operation in 1954 and RFs took over in 1968, only to be replaced by BNs in 1974. GS 65 was based at Hertford garage from January 1963 to June 1968 and following a period of storage was sold for scrap in July 1969. (Michael Wickham collection)

An unusual combination of blinds is displayed by RT 981 in this view taken on 3 July 1975 in Hitchin. The 303C was a new route introduced by LCBS on 14 October 1972 requiring two Stevenage-based RTs to operate Monday to Friday peak hour journeys between Hitchin and Stevenage Industrial Estate. The RTs were replaced by spare RP coaches following reductions to the 716 Green Line service in May 1976. However, RT 981 struck lucky because it returned to public service at Reigate between May 1977 and February 1978 having been re-certificated. The vehicle then served as a trainer at various garages. After withdrawal in February 1981 it was sold and has since been preserved. (Peter Plummer)

With the increase in Country Bus services arising from the further expansion of new towns, a different bus route series was started using 8xx numbers as there were few vacant numbers in the 3xx and 4xx series. Route 800 was introduced in Stevenage on 29 July 1964 to complement existing route 801, operating a circular service around Stevenage in the reverse direction and then onwards to Hitchin or Martins Wood or Sishes End. Occasionally, it was necessary to draft in some red RTs for a short time to supplement a brief shortage of green ones. For example, this happened between January and March 1966, as evidenced in this view of two grubby RTs, Green Line-liveried RT 3237 and red RT 2912, at Stevenage bus station in March 1966. The reign of RTs on Stevenage's local services ended with the arrival of ANs, their replacement on route 800 taking place in October 1972. (Peter Plummer collection)

The vehicles for phase one of the Superbus services consisted of five Swifts (SMs 495-499) and two Metro-Scanias (MSs 1 and 2). In this 1972 view Green Line-liveried RP 27 pulls out of Stevenage garage past MS 2 which is heading a line of RTs. This garage, located in Danestrete, was opened in 1959 and closed in 1991. A supermarket now occupies the site. The 1959 garage replaced one which opened at Fishers Green in 1955. Hatfield-based RP 27 started as a trainer in January 1972 and entered service on routes 716 and 716A on 11 March 1972, replacing RMCs. It was withdrawn in June 1983 and sold but was subsequently destroyed in the same depot fire that claimed RP 53 seen earlier. (C Carter/Online Transport Archive)

Stevenage was the first of the post-war "New Towns" and generated several additional routes to serve the new housing and industrial estates. Some of these were subject to radical alteration with the introduction of novel, experimental services from 29 December 1969, starting with the Blue Arrow "personal taxis". On 20 March 1971, the first of Stevenage's Swifts arrived to replace RTs on route 809, a route which was soon advertised as providing the "No Fuss Bus". This 1972 view of the bus station depicts SM 483 and an RT in traditional livery while, in between, SM 497 carries the Superbus canary yellow and oxford blue colours chosen by local residents for the subsidised services which were introduced from 31 July 1971. (C Carter/Online Transport Archive)

The 716A Green Line service (Woking-Stevenage via Marble Arch) was relatively short lived, being introduced on 5 October 1955 and ceasing on 14 May 1976. From the following day, the 716 routeing was changed to include the Woking to Welwyn Garden City section of the 716A. The route was operated out of Addlestone and Hatfield garages, whose RMCs were replaced by RPs on 11 March 1972 arising from OPO conversion. This photograph of Addlestone-based RP 23 was taken in March 1973 at Hatfield garage. This opened in 1959, more closely reflecting the New Town image than the original 1922-built General garage. However, even the new garage has since closed and no trace remains. RP 23 has also ceased to exist following its withdrawal and subsequent sale in June 1983. (Peter Plummer collection)

Here is a view of Green Line route 716 in Stevenage when RMCs were in charge, before OPO conversion using RPs. This route, like many others, underwent several changes in latter days. When this late 1960s picture of RMC 1513 was taken outside the fire station in St George's Way the 716 operated from Chertsey to Hitchin. In 1976 the southern destination was changed to Woking and in 1978 cross-London working was abandoned, the service being curtailed to operate only between Woking and Oxford Circus. The 716 was withdrawn in 1980 but RMC 1513 lives on as an active member of the heritage fleet belonging to Ensignbus. In July 1979 it had been repurchased by LT from LCBS and was eventually painted red with gold relief to operate the Express X15 service. That is the livery which it carries today. (Alan Mortimer)

This view of a seemingly abandoned RT 4738 with passengers aboard destined for South Hatfield has stopped opposite Hatfield bus garage for a crew change. This location in St Albans Road East is completely unrecognisable today. Apart from the demolition of the Addo office block in the distance and the bus garage on the north side of the road, the buildings behind the bus on the south side, including the old General bus garage, have also disappeared, making way for a sunken commercial development. RT 4738 was allocated to Hatfield from August 1965 to June 1971 and was withdrawn in August 1976, going for scrap a few months later.
(John Herting/Online Transport Archive)

Standing in Hertford's large open air bus station is Routemaster coach RMC 1505, looking as though it has recently returned from its repaint in October 1970 following its demotion to bus work. Sadly, the gloss soon wore off because when it was resold to LT in January 1978 it was immediately dispatched for dismantling and scrapping. In this view passengers are on board ready for the bus to set off on its short journey working route 395A. This route went from Fanham Common in Ware to Sele Farm Estate in Hertford. The bus station in Market Street was opened in 1935 and closed in 1980. A replacement bus station of smaller proportions but similarly exposed has been built in Bircherley Road. (John Herting/Online Transport Archive)

Entering Green Line service in November 1965, RC 8 is reduced in this view to working Hertford Local Service 333, yet still retains its Green Line livery as it picks up passengers outside the shops in The Avenue, Molewood Estate, on 17 August 1974. This route witnessed increasingly large buses, from Leyland Cubs to Leyland Nationals with GSs and RFs in between. Thirteen RCs were transferred to Hertford for bus use in 1974, representing the entire class except RC 11 which had previously caught fire on route 711 and was burnt out. All the RCs were withdrawn between 1977 and 1979 and scrapped. Route 333 continues to serve Molewood Estate, operated by Centrebus. (Mike Harris)

Spare a thought for any motorist, pedestrian or equestrian approaching this corner and being unexpectedly confronted with a bus! Route 386 operated on certain days of the week linking various villages and hamlets with Hitchin, Stevenage, Hertford and Bishops Stortford. During the course of the journey the vehicle would travel along several narrow lanes including this one near Ardeley as it heads for Cottered and onwards to Bishops Stortford on 27 July 1974. Thanks to the very co-operative driver of RF 220, the photographer was able to hop-off the bus without getting run-over and climb back on again. RF 220 arrived at Hertford garage in June 1970 and remained there until withdrawal in September 1974, whereupon it was sold for scrap. BNs replaced RFs on this route from 22 February 1975. (Mike Harris)

The 386 was a long rambling route and this view dating from July 1974 depicts RF 220 again, this time passing the Nag's Head in the hamlet of Wellpond Green, near Standon. In April 1954, when the Hertford-based buses for the 386 also worked the 329, three GSs replaced two RFs and a 10T10. In October 1958 the Sunday service was withdrawn and RFs regained possession of the service. Over the years the working of the 386 varied. Before the Sunday service was withdrawn the entire route was only worked at weekends and part-worked solely on Tuesdays (Hitchin to Buntingford) and Thursdays (Buntingford to Bishops Stortford), although there were some additional short workings. (Mike Harris)

On 21 June 1975, in an unchanged setting today, RT 4550 swings into Epping LT station approach from Station Road on its journey to Harlow from the Ford Motor Company's HQ in Eagle Way, Warley, Brentwood. This bus was based at Harlow from May 1973 to September 1975, at which point it was withdrawn and sold for scrap in February 1976. RTs were replaced on the 339 and dispersed elsewhere when the ten borrowed Southend PD3s started arriving from 29 March 1976. These were returned to Southend from 29 January 1977 at which point RMLs took over the route. Interestingly, it is currently still possible to travel on the 339 by RT or Routemaster over part of the route as a result of the London Bus Company providing a periodic service in conjunction with the Epping Ongar Railway. (Peter Plummer)

Well-loaded ex-Green Line coach, RCL 2240, hurries along Rush Green Road (A125) at Roneo Corner, Romford, having passed The Crown, a hostelry which is still open today. The location takes its name from the defunct Roneo office equipment company's factory which was built in 1907. Roneo was known world wide for its printing machines (duplicators) until these were superseded by photocopiers. Route 370 operated out of Grays garage and ran from Romford to Tilbury Ferry. RCLs supplanted RMCs on this service in February 1973 and were in turn replaced by BTs (Bristol VRTs) in June 1977, albeit crew operated until becoming OPO in the following month. RCL 2240, seen here clinging on to its Green Line livery, was downgraded to a bus in 1972, repurchased by LT in July 1979, converted to open top in 1991 and sold to a brewery in 2000. (David Christie)

Before the replacement of Grays' RTs by demoted RMCs on route 370 which mainly occurred between January and March 1972, RT 4733 represents the old order as it passes St Laurence church in Corbets Tey Road, Upminster, on 4 May 1968. The 370 was a long established service between Romford and Grays with, at one time, projections to Purfleet. On 2 January 1952 it was extended from Grays to Tilbury Ferry, absorbing Eastern National's 37A service. This was a consequence of LT taking over thirteen local Eastern National services in the Grays area on 30 September 1951. RT 4733 spent from March 1967 until June 1971 at Grays whereupon it was withdrawn and sold for scrap. (W Ryan)

Green RTs could fraternise regularly in several locations with green RLHs but meeting a red RLH in service was far less common. In this view dating from 1970, RT 4481 is turning into Corbets Tey Road from St Mary's Lane by St Laurence church in Upminster on route 370. There it passes RLH 69 from the Central Area's Hornchurch garage, substituting for a red RT on the six minute long, single bus peak hour 248A service. 18 September 1970 was the last day for Hornchurch's RLHs and after transfer to Dalston RLH 69 was withdrawn in April 1971 and exported to the USA. It was repatriated in 2012 along with RLHs 53 and 71 and is now owned by the London Bus Company. In contrast, RT 4481 did not fare well. It served at Grays from March 1966 until withdrawal in June 1971 and was then sold for scrap. The backdrop of this photograph is unchanged today apart from the ownership of the shops. (David Christie)

This picture taken in bleak surroundings depicts LT's most easterly route, the 349 from Grays to Coryton via Stanford-le-Hope, Corringham and Shell Haven. This last-named place, visited here by RT 3242 in 1968, had been an established port on the Thames Estuary and latterly, until closure in 1999, the location of an oil refinery which, by coincidence, belonged to Shell. The 349 had previously been Eastern National's route 35. In the mid-1930s LT had even briefly operated a Grays to Shell Haven service because it came as part of LT's takeover of local operator, Day and Bedingfield on 1 August 1934. In addition to the limited frequency 349 service, Shell Haven was also served by some independent bus operators as well as Shell's own bus fleet carrying its own employees. RT 3242 worked at Grays from April 1968 to January 1972 and was withdrawn in July of that year. (John Herting/Online Transport Archive)

Route 323 did the rounds of various housing estates on its journey from Grays, visiting Uplands Estate, Woodside Estate and Chadwell St Mary's Brentwood Road Estate where this picture of RF 687 in Alexandra Close was taken in June 1975. In the following month the RF was withdrawn and sold for scrap, thus ending its five year stint at Grays. Leyland Nationals started to take over the service from RFs in February 1976 but, as crew operation on other Grays routes was still prevalent and there was some spare capacity, RCLs were allocated some off-peak services on the 323 from April 1976. (Mike Harris)

Grays' RF 687 (see previous page) seems to have been kept busy in its last month of service because this photograph shows it on route 371B in Byron Gardens, Tilbury, also in June 1975. Until October 1969 this service had been operated by RTs, at which point conversion to OPO took place, using RFs. Grays' fleet of RTs were eliminated in early 1972 following the arrival of displaced Green Line Routemasters but until then, RTs did sometimes supplement the RFs on the 371B. Leyland Nationals replaced RFs on the 371B in February 1976 but the route was withdrawn on 3 April 1976 as part of a major re-organisation of LCBS services in the Grays area. (John Miller)

The final picture in this book is taken at the Bata Shoe factory at East Tilbury. In fact this was more than a factory, it was a small town in itself, given the extensive facilities provided. The 367, represented here in June 1975 by Grays-based RCL 2247, was a Monday-Friday peak hour service from Tilbury Docks intended mainly for Bata factory workers. Behind the RCL is a Bristol Lodekka belonging to Eastern National operating route 245. This was another Monday-Friday peak hour works service, this time starting from Basildon. Ex-Green Line coach RCL 2247 was downgraded to a bus and sent to Grays in 1972. It was withdrawn there in October 1978 and immediately re-purchased by LT who operated the vehicle until December 1984 before selling it for scrap. (Mike Harris)